Forehanding and Backhanding- If You're Lucky

Words by
Gary Paulsen

Pictures by
Heinz Kluetmeier

ᴘ Childrens Press

Library of Congress Number: 77-27046

1 2 3 4 5 6 7 8 9 0 82 81 80 79 78

Printed in the United States of America.

Library of Congress Cataloging in Publication Data

Paulsen, Gary.
    Forehanding and backhanding—if you're lucky.

    Summary: A humorous commentary on different aspects
of tennis using photographs of professional players.
    1. Tennis—Juvenile literature. I. Kluetmeier,
Heinz. II. Title.
GV996.5.P38   796.34'22   77-27046
ISBN 0-8172-1158-6 lib. bdg.

TENNIS

Tennis is a game played by two or four people on a rectangular court.

The players use a mesh racket to slam a furry ball back and forth until somebody misses.

When this happens the winner gets fifteen points and the loser gets nothing.

But they call it *love,* instead of nothing.

A lot of people don't completely understand tennis.

SERVE

Serving is the first thing you learn in tennis.

This is when you slam the furry little ball over the net for the first time.

Form is very important in serving.

Follow-through is everything when it comes to the form of your serve.

Even when you miss the ball.

But you don't get extra points for pointing at the ball when it goes by.

Some people think jumping in the air and wiggling your legs helps the follow-through.

Or making a sad face.

Of course waiting for the serve
is important too.

You should get into a ready, defensive
crouch. Then make sure the official is
watching you.

Hopefully, the official can see you
from under his hat.

One of the most important parts of the
serve is remembering to let go of the ball.

Before you hit it with the racket.

Otherwise you're going to have little
squares all over the back of your hand.

FOREHAND

There are two ways to "answer" the serve. Two ways to slam it back across the net so the other player misses it and you win.

They are the *forehand* and the *backhand*.

Actually there are three ways to answer a serve. But nobody likes to watch a player duck and cover his head.

The forehand is when you swing the racket around in front of you hard enough to make your eyes cross.

Of course there are many different kinds
of forehand.

There is the pinched-mouth forehand.

The falling-over-backward forehand.

And there is the well known why-me forehand.

Or, when all others fail, the classic
cry-in-the-towel forehand. When you miss.

Now and then a player will try the rare kneel-on-the-ground forehand.

But only if the ball is very high and coming down very fast.

And only when the player doesn't have time to dig a hole and cover his head.

A "sizzler" is when the serve is coming so fast it can't be stopped.

Some sizzlers seem to smoke when they go by.

Sometimes the only thing to do with a sizzler is cover your head and hope that it misses you.

Some sizzlers go by so fast they knock
you around and flip you in the air.

Then the only thing you can do is hold
your racket out and hope the ball hits it.

Of course, this won't win matches.

But you *will* stay alive.

Another way to return serves with a forehand is to hold onto the ball, change into a costume, and fool your opponent.

Just make sure your tennis socks match your skirt.

And bonnet.

BACKHAND

The backhand is the exact opposite of the forehand. To do the backhand properly you just bring the racket from the rear with a powerful swinging motion that slams the ball back at your opponent.

It helps if you keep your eye on the ball.

And if your legs don't curl up under you.

23

Many players consider the backhand the most difficult part of tennis.

Some will even chase the ball until they can use their backhand.

Sometimes they get it right.

Others may try kicking the ground. Now and then a player will close her eyes and go by "feel."

But it doesn't help.

Even poking your racket into the dirt
won't help.

The ground doesn't have any better
backhand than you do.

Probably the most important thing about a good backhand is getting the right stance.

Run to where the ball is coming and get your feet positioned correctly.

Then look angry, grit your teeth, and *swing*!

Then try not to look surprised when
you miss.

In fact, most of good tennis is trying to
not look surprised when you miss.